VELOCITY

I've lived my whole life in a perpetual state of going, going, gone.

Our interactions are glances

Making contact collision at a red-light traffic stop

I saw that deep breath you took

In your exhale,

I saw your life moving fast track by

As if it were a train car, and yeah,

I feel it, too.

Sometimes at intersections,

I often envision another car slamming into mine.

Folding my speculative life like an aluminum can

Crushing me like a response to

"You looked.

You didn't see me."

My imagination is a silhouette reaper.

My death comes in night sweat flashes

But I don't find it that grim.

My self-fulfilling prophecy of abandon

I've got that deafening tone

Right before I call you to action,

But you're already gone.

Now I'm seeing most of my investments,

Didn't come close to breaking even.

Can you see me?

If I seem angry,

You know

I'm just disappointed

And if I seem bitter,

You know.

I was six the first time

The Earth's crust split between my two light up sneakers

I folded it back and tried to catch that glimpse of molten...

Nothing.

Ever since then,

I don't find existence comfortable

Unless I'm sweating

My heart audibly thudding against its cage

It's failed attempt at escape

Near constant chaos is carried around like

Virtuous epiphany

Maybe you didn't see me.

Making love in silence

Starting house fires while wearing blind folds

To see who could get out of the exit first

And man, the last time we played hide-&-go seek

You really found the best place

Way back,

In the depths of my memory

I've made paper-mache voodoo dolls of myself

In attempt to make myself weightless

And shredded it to pieces when it didn't work

I blamed myself

When you didn't see me

Flash to a scene

A bar

That moment of silence

When you go to lift a shot to your lips

Bliss anticipation with a dose of angst

That's my favorite spot

Uncomfortable

I don't even like straight liquor

A break in noise and speed to my someday, hopefully,

Quiet comatose head

Preparing for a night you know will play out

Just like the last time

Hoping maybe tonight will be different

Maybe tonight will bring transparency

Maybe tonight

They see me

It's false and you know that

But what is a wish if not a stretch?

A wish that this life isn't just moving

Blindly by

I don't want to spend my time here as a ghost

If we return to molten nothing

Let's spend these blinking seconds

As me

At a traffic stop

Seeing you

To the Girl Who I Said, "Be Part of my Revolution, My Revelation",

And Then I Never Spoke to Again

You looked up at me with large brown eyes like I walked across water to meet you

Like you had been waiting for me

At a bus stop

To come and bring you purpose

In the form of purple polish and girlish giggles

I pulled up and you got in without asking any questions

I am always waiting on your questions

Questions like

"What the fuck am I doing here?"

You said you always like how I stammered and talked in third person

Like I wasn't actually present in my own life, so -

A couldn't take a second to notice that your fingertips

They dripped with honey

And that you, you were looking for your own questions

Her phone was buzzing almost as much as her head

A gave you a made-up name, so you played the right part

In her modern rom com day dream

What I mean to say is

Inside me is like a violent noon on a fall day

A day like October 2nd

When it's chilly but you can still taste popsicles

And chlorine, and your tan line is not yet faded

We hadn't come to terms with the fact

That there was no more swimming or shorts

Soon, we'd be carving

And it'd last all winter

I careen less wildly

In fashion, squinting through a blindfold

Like I know what I am doing

And you believed that I did

I kept acting like it was possible

For me to ever love you

I wanted to believe it was

Because you kissed like fireworks

And you had your shit together

I mean like, really together

You intimidated me more than I'll ever actually tell you

Only because I carry my successes around in a pack of cigarettes

In my back pocket

And some cheap lines I only have the courage to say

After the second drink

Did I get too high that one night, when you finally decided I wasn't going to show up?

I was sitting beside you

You were studying my face this time for answers

Window down

The music in my car was so damn good

I've heard it a thousand times,

Yet I'll still turn it up every time

And rewind often

Just like the lover sneaking into my room

Every night I told you goodbye

Knowing I wouldn't sleep

Neither would you

Your grandmother called you her *barajo'*

I couldn't understand why you seemed so grounded

When the questions you wanted to ask

Were out of reach

Near close to my lack of reach for you

And I'm not sorry

For the first time, I'm practicing not owning anything but myself

Forgive me when you find the time

Here is an answer,

I doubt it's what you wanted

But I'm sticking to it cause it's all I've got

Where I'm from

Fall only lasts about a week

Blasé Faire of Fair

I think your idea of sleeping with me started

As a broken down, re-run,

Great conquest calamity

I think you then decided you would keep me

Because you've never seen a woman

Make a cannon out of a cracked voice

To the elongated side of a closed door

You never asked if I was for sale

You didn't check transactional history

You didn't see the signatures are only

Crushed poppy seeds

The previous patrons hide away in a cellar

You, hollow gaze mercenary

You can't compete or complete that

Which is whole

By casting shadows in limelight

You did not happen to me

Any more than an afternoon

On a forgettable Tuesday

Five clock strike summers ago

We never spoke in all the words

We exchanged

Between clumsy clamoring movements

In a windless inferno

Me,

Queen-chaos,

Queen-vague,

Queen-quick-run-away

You're a one night stand

That turned into day, after day, after day

How many times did I slam vodka

Cocktails you purchased

Both of us hoping

It would make your existence in my life

Synonymous with euphoria

How many times did you empty

Your eyelids on my ever-growing fainter backside

Hoping I might turn around?

The only question I still have for you

Is the same one I asked you

Weeks ago

When I awoke to your tumultuous volumes

Coming up my wood creak stairway

What are you still doing here?

I've never really been that fair

My lips, a one-line zinger

Like a bent arrow back pull firing squad

My lips

Won't fall faintly on the nothingness

Between our ice capped peaks

You're statuesque

And you know that

And while I watch your crude fingers struggle shake

To lite a match

I become a little less concerned with "pretty"

Despite my efforts

In juice and meat

There's no sweetness in an orange peel

To summarize, and quickly –

I'm not answering the phone anymore

This never has been, and never will be

HANGING ON RED/READ

You say

Nostalgia is death

Until pointed, specific

A reminder and a lesson.

So, tell me about how you try

Desperately to relive every moment,

Every mistake,

Cracking your knees on error error, no trial

Chasing the dark tunnel of extortion

Faith -

Once looked so good on you

Your windpipes are concave

Where is your voice, boy?

Where is your shaking fist

and all gut drive thirst?

Chin down

Third time this week

You drag that rope

Up my cement steps

To that noose around your neck

Hoping today is the day I can finally untie

That knot

But you've moved glass between us

My beloved comrade,

Once battle beau enigma,

That tree you've chosen

It is time you look at it

The branches -

Corroded

Nothing grows here, termite season

Thousands of men have died in this place

The choice not theirs

Martyrs unremembered

An epitaph to an unmarked grave

In the soil, their legacy

Ours to inherit

Why choose today,

To make tomorrow forever's static?

Your complacency -

Does not alleviate

Your cowardice never brought pleasure

Are you tired?

Good, there's no rest stop near

Keep up, move forward

STOP

Listen to the wind

(It does not hear you back)

Stop sitting in sewage

If you're going to ask why you stink

There's no keeping record time

To a vinyl stuck on skip

Quit the fit

There is so much more

Than your drunken delirium of bullshit

Bring the passion

Firm — and so fucking tender

Effervescent but a shimmer

I want to see you tremble again

Drive your teeth into this

Embrace another side

Wistful paradise

Apathy is no match

For my drum roll beat pulse

The world – burns and churns

Pull back the curtains

Rip down the blinds

Revolution will bring a crimson horizon

"History is ours!

And people make history"

We can fracture reality

Dissemble and disarm

Until stardust is a child's wishes

And rust settles on a crescent dagger

The hands of the clock

Are rapid fire jeopardy wheels

To a budding soon blossomed quake

So now go

Put on your best suit

Prepare your plane wreck face

ASSUMING FORM

Bouncing amoeba

Holy entropy

Walk with me

Amor Fati!

Golden ghost

Forbidden analogies

Forever pathed in front of me

Born of blood

Blood-borne

Pathogenic // inseparable

Is the sorceress from me

Attrition, now history

Sun-bleached and gracious

Voiceless, and eternally reoccurring

Hands cupped like youth fountain

Hands cupped like thighs – a goblet

Hands cupped like yes, drink from them

Insatiable hysteria

This could be

Tomorrow, never be

I CHOOSE CHANCE!

Diagnosed sickening wild-eyed stars above

Wrap whispered opportunity

Like a scarf, around me

Like a breeze, all around me

Like a shudder, inside me

I am everything I want to be

And I am equally everything,

Everything

I don't see

Cast // ignite

Subjectively // seductively

Tongue birthed language

Language birthed fiction

Fiction birthed war

Born of blood

Blood-borne, violently

The center of the body

Uncensored

Lies the

Inertia of my fluvial formality

FIVE AVOIDABLE AND PREDICTIVE MISTAKES (I LIVED OUT ANYWAY)

CONCLUSION TO BE DETERMINED

1. When I was two, I went to go hit a dog with a stick. A big dog. It tore my head open.

2. When I chugged whiskey to keep up with the boys (who I did not like, but I liked the idea of them liking me) my adolescent lack of tolerance was not the only thing I shelved. Later I swallowed.

3. Cocaine abuse and starvation evidently leads to nose bleeds and fatigue.

4. When I told my all-American, saint mother that I am a communist, her face morphed more into that of a stranger than the day I told her I've enjoyed sex with women, or that drugs replace memories, or that I have yet to feel the presence of her god.

5. When I got back to town from impossible escape, la paloma looked for me. Praised me and hunted me, a black rhinoceros, I caved into desires, sting of absence growing sharper – You make a beast out of a woman, and she'll kill you just to see you on your knees.

6. Did I mention there's six? For a moment suspended in time, I believed bringing a child into this screaming world, together, meant you'd look at me the same way I looked at the sky – ya know – before you flattened me on my back and said "look scared straight". I sort of wish it were a metaphor.

My bookshelf is crammed with books I will only ever read the first five chapters of.

Kind of like how my backside is covered with the faces of lovers I have long since forgotten.

I bore too easy. The character lacks complexity. I just found something better – it's not you.

It is me.

I wanted to be consistent. I found a therapist.

I haven't seen her in weeks. She told me I'm too quick wit. That I don't need her, but

She likes my fraudulent mind play. Deny, deny, deny, keep moving.

She could not see I was reaching out a cup for spare change and she handed me a counterfeit hundred.

Everyone likes to hear "you don't need me".

I digress, to underdress my wounds.

I am "better" – what that means, most days

I'm a model figurine wrapped in cellophane.

Embodying mutilated femme.

My left hand holds a white flag – splattered

You decide by what.

I count bones in my graveyard and their presence is ever-so comforting.

I still stay up at night,

Tonight, I'll read past the fifth chapter.

This year, my birthday present to myself was to stop walking around like there's a thorn in my foot.

If you plant roses at every exit,

You will bleed every time you leave.

Some things I cannot predict.

I write the most when I'm so hungover I can't think about anything but

That single emotion of pseudo-regret

Maybe it's introspection.

Anyway

I do not feel much – often

I can tell my family's concern in the distance they keep

The consequential headache of my choices is the only time I can cry.

My vices are street lights to insipid avenues paved in bricks of blue.

I didn't think I'd pay for any of it

I didn't ask for any of it

Struggle for it

I'm repaying it by bringing life to a girl who still never asks for more than...

Everything

In interest

With ruptured lungs and toothy grins,

I'll give it all to her

Even if it's contingent on parting the sky

Once, I asked for sanctuary

And fruitful dignity

I was given a daughter

Little she asks me why

All my responses are mute, if not flat and dry

What I cannot tell her today,

Is I have all this inside me, behind me,

And I still don't know

In her own predictive mistakes and sixth chapters,

She might not either

A ballad of continuously uncharted territory,

We will create conviction

Making a lifeline out of a tight rope

Stretched hovering over shoreline crashing

Learning to carry the lightness of this living

I WON HER IN A LIGHTNING STRIKE!

(OR MAYBE A CARD GAME)

It's another night of not sleep

I can hear my neighbors throwing an array of dishes at each other again

They scream

In familiarity

Of fragility

I wonder if they noticed

Yesterday

The wide-eyed girl pounding on my door

Ringing the bell over, over and again

Knowing he was in my bed upstairs

The night before we broke into my old home

Our old home

By the river

Taking with us a mug of cucumber vodka

A likely false notion of nostalgia

Our shoes filled with ever accelerated hysteria

I have thoughts about my place

In your story,

Pigeon

But I can't find an eraser in the jumbles of

Pens and brushes

Stuffed into the art desk we fought over

You texted me that you're sorry

You are sick

Like that hasn't been revealed in years of

Flesh fights and battle cries

See, I'd make you soup

But my landlord still needs to fix my stove

And it's not the only heat under construction

They say we reap what we sew

Now you're reaping

Everywhere you go

In smirks and hidden pearls of mouth

Pretending they can offer any promises

You make a prophet out of me

Forever yours, pillar of salt girl

Like as though my fuck will provide the key

From the cage

That is yourself

And all that you touch

Which mostly consists of whiskey pints

And the thighs of young women

Who couldn't possibly know any better

But the lies

Bittersweet

The ones you don't tell me

Are so exquisite the girls will weep

So will the glasses in which your lips meet

My pool of forgiveness

Is your favorite place to bathe

You've thought hard on how the water is so clear

When last week you rinsed off transgressions

Of blood, of mud, of boyhood

You can't find our end

I can't place a point of begin

Like the coordinates to our symphony

Got lost in all the tragedy

It's parasitic symmetry

You've never known how to quit

For me –

Quitting is my first flight, maybe fight?

Response to every question

Even the ones I stopped asking

Do you remember that night?

At the saloon

I climbed on all fours to glimpse my own reflection

Moving backwards

You were bangin' on rooftops

In a foreign city

We cried to that one song

Wait -

What song?

A façade

A time trick

We're trying desperately

To purchase more of it

Mints of the forgotten

The commodity to our panic waltz

His fingertips say,

"Look, babe, if my love isn't torture,

I'm going to teach you to hate proper."

Not knowing that grace

Is found in the fire

He's gone tone deaf

He doesn't hear the congregation shouting

It was all a mistranslation

Church is not eternal

It is internal

And he should know by now

I'm not afraid to die

Or disappear

It's always been my bee

My best quality

Loneliness

Is the only thing I've ever been able to count on one hand

No

One finger

It is the only thing that precedes me

I keep telling myself

Every choice is the right choice

Ridden in solipsism

I can no longer count the number of times

You left

And ran back

You're stuck

Like a rotating door

Your love, a game of musical chairs

My fears are stacked against me

Like building blocks to my wall

Of self-deprecation

The fear at the center

The one at point blank

Like a loaded revolver

Guided misfire

Is my fear of you finally learning

How to live

After me

Untitled A

My knuckles are splitting

Underwear still itching

It's digging into my hip bones

Like a knife licking –

Bootstrap

My nerves unturned

I wasn't born for long hair

Or clipped fingernails

Mostly sticker weed chuck wars

And atomic putrid dancing

Sapphic supreme

Burn it down

Don't stop

Scream

Untitled B

Trembling

In the shower

Hot tears

I yell at you

I yell at my father

I yell at centuries of the commodification of my body

Of my will

Demanding forgiving

I throw up

He came back for me

For humanity

To reintegrate and reattribute mortality

He left

Again and again and again

For years

For the next best thing

For a fuck

For a breath

He ran

For his life

Forgetting he gave mine to me

How do you tell God to stay?

Invalidating the daughter in me

The daughter after me

The woman, witch, bitch

I would be

You're forsaken and no part of me

I'm closing your cupboard door

I am no longer psyche

Fuck your garden

Fruit unborn without the woman

Without we

"...the voice of a body dancing, laughing, shrieking, crying. Whose is it? It is, they say, the voice of a woman, newborn and yet archaic, a voice of milk and blood, a voice silenced but savage."

The Newly Born Woman
Introduction: A Tarantella of Theory, S. M. Gilbert

www.ingramcontent.com/pod-product-compliance
Lightning Source LLC
Chambersburg PA
CBHW071123220526
45467CB00004B/2025